Forgivin

Judith Crane

Vicar of Blackwell and Tibshelf, Derbyshire

GROVE BOOKS LIMITED

RIDLEY HALL RD CAMBRIDGE CB3 9HU

Contents

Acknowledgments

Thanks to all who have offered support, challenge and encouragement along the way, especially Bill Broderick SJ.

The Cover Illustration is after Michelangelo's 'Creation of Adam'

First Impression August 2004
ISSN 0262-799X
ISBN 1 85174 570 X

A Spirituality for the Suffering   1

Anyone embarked upon the spiritual journey is, sooner or later, going to come up against the memory of painful events in their lives.

For some of these they may bear no responsibility. These events may simply have been one specific occasion or a set of continuing circumstances; either way, they will have had a profound impact upon the soul. For some, this impact may have been turned to good already. For others, growth may have been stunted by the knowledge that the so-called God of Love has allowed them to suffer in the way they have.

Historically, the teaching and preaching of Christian faith has often given the impression that the God we worship is both all-powerful, all-knowing and beyond questioning on the one hand, and all-loving and protective of the faithful soul on the other. It is God who forgives the sinner, not the other way about. Not surprisingly, this produces a huge tension in the wounded heart, a conflict that refuses any further progress on the spiritual journey until proper attention is paid to it.

This, then, is a spirituality of those who have suffered in childhood in some way, particularly through abuse of some kind. It is a spirituality of the victim, though not of course the only such spirituality. And, it may also be helpful for the chronically ill, the disabled or the cruelly bereaved—anyone who knows a suffering that they have not invited and cannot be blamed for, though the sufferer often does blame herself. This is the story not just of one person but of many people, whose journeys with God have this common factor of blameless suffering. Their stories are brought together in this telling as one composite journey, so as to avoid breaking confidences. The universal experience of suffering is told in a particular and personal narrative style which may at times be tough going, but which can hold worthwhile rewards.

> *This is the spirituality of those who have suffered in childhood in some way, particularly through abuse of some kind*

Language of course is a problem. I use 'she' for the victim and 'he' for the abuser, but this is only linguistic convenience. I am well aware that women also abuse emotionally, physically and sexually, and that boys are also victims of either gender. Statistically, however, male abusers and female victims are numerically greater. Similarly, I sometimes use the masculine pronoun for God, because this is a traditional rendering, and to use the feminine can draw attention to itself in a distracting manner. For some this may cause real difficulties in view of the above, though I hope not to the extent that it renders this text unacceptable. Secondly, my use of Scripture is devotional. It rests on the assumption that everything in Scripture is present by the gift and intention of God, whether I like it or not, or can live by what it says—it is there to be wrestled with in prayer and in life. There is no space here for academic discussion, only for personal engagement.

Thirdly, this booklet is about the need to come to terms with God for the suffering that has been experienced at a personal level, and while this will often include an imperative need to forgive other human beings, that is not the primary object of attention here.

What is the Problem?

This is the story of a journey. It is the journey from the surface to the depths. It is the journey from faith held only in the conscious parts of the mind, to faith which holds and integrates the soul in wholeness. It is the journey towards real peace and real joy. Imagine a child, infant or older, male or female, whose trust is destroyed by the physical or psychological attack of an adult; whose body may have been violated or damaged, whose relational life is always thereafter a complicated and uncertain endeavour; who becomes the bearer of shame and humiliation well into her adult life. You know this person; she sits next to you in the pew, you see her in your congregation on Sunday and at work on Monday. She is in a committed relationship or she is alone. She is a mother or she is childless. Her life may look good, apparently functioning well, or she may be obviously in the depths of despair, unable even to get out of bed in the mornings.

It is the journey from faith held only in the conscious parts of the mind, to faith which holds and integrates the soul in wholeness

There is no way of knowing who she is from the outside, but you will know people like the wounded one whose story is told here, for there are many of us. It may even be you.

There are hundreds, thousands of women, and men, whose earliest life-stories are tales of continuing intimidation and violence, or of one-off acts of rape or other assaults. Children who have been used by adults as if they were things, not people; used for pleasure or for the relief of the frustrations and fears of an adult. They are the six year old whose only experience of loving touch was a violation of her private parts: they are the nine year old whose male relatives used her for sexual relief, and whose female relatives ignored her distress: they are the twelve year old bewildered by her teacher's sexual interest in her: they are the fifteen year old attacked by a stranger on the way home from school. They are the ones whose suffering has been buried out of sight for no-one was there to help them at the time. They are those who are making the best of things, but whose misery and anger sometimes erupts into their everyday lives in spite of themselves. They are the ones who have been labelled workaholic or alcoholic, depressed or anorexic, and they are the ones nobody has noticed enough to give them a label at all.

The problem which such grown-up children face when they are Christians, but may well be unable to articulate, is *how can the Christian account of God bring me the healing I need?* Finding the answer to this question is the journey that has to be made by the wounded. It is a question which has to be answered within the psychological reality of the wounded one's own life. What she has accepted as a cosmic truth—a truth 'out there'—

Statements of the healing and redemptive love of God must move from the abstract to the highly personal

must also be a truth capable of demonstration within her own spiritual experience—a truth 'in here.' It is her personal Christian faith which is on the line. Statements of the healing and redemptive love of God must move from the abstract to the highly personal. It is no good just saying these things. If the wounded one cannot know at least the potential for healing in this life, then she is likely to dismiss doctrinal claims as untrue. The calling of such wounded people is to find within their own felt experience the reality both of crucifixion and of resurrection, and then to live out this truth in their subsequent lives. It is not enough that the Bible says God loves you; the wounded one needs to know in her own experience that she is beloved. Her wounds have left her with powerful feelings, many of which cannot yet be named, but surely the love and healing of God can meet those feelings?

2

Who is God?

The beginning of this risky and pain-filled journey comes when the dissonance between what is held intellectually and what is really believed in the hidden parts of the soul is exposed.

There is a shift in the interior landscape which announces the movement of the Spirit, a kind of earthquake, a tremor which shakes the surface of life. It is the movement towards integration and integrity, the gifts of God.

The very ground under the feet of the wounded one is shaking. All that she has depended upon for safety seems to be shifting within her, and this may also be happening in the outward circumstances of her life too. There may be bereavement or redundancy, family or financial worries, all of which add to the sense of insecurity she begins to feel, as she wonders where God is in her life. The risk of faith becomes very real for the one who accepts the invitation to growth and healing from God. This 'riskiness' often makes the wounded one rather threatening to churches and church-people. In any case, she will project outwards her own dread of her inner turbulence, and may need much reassurance from others that she is not as disturbing to others as she is to herself. Because she needs space to voice doubt and fury, and to acknowledge her sometimes 'unacceptable' views of God, she will not survive a worshipping community that rigidly insists on continuous orthodoxy in speech and action among its members. A church that has a robust trust in the mysterious movements of God and a hospitality which affirms individual human worth will offer a secure religious environment in which the questions caused by the pain may be worked through.

But how can anyone who has known the personal destructiveness of events for which they were not responsible hold an image of God which is helpful and truthful?

The answer is that the wounded one cannot, at the outset. Her image of God may be one-dimensional—God is either not there at all, or, God behaves in

> *God is what require God to be, and any indication to the contrary must be shoved away out of sight*

such an unloving and immoral way that this God cannot possibly be worshipped and followed. This is the favourite avoidance expressed within western society at present: the insistence that God must measure up to what I require in a God or I will have nothing to do with him.

Or, her image of God may be two-dimensional—the bright shiny face of faith that speaks of love, joy and peace in God, while there is a hidden obverse that is dark, uncaring and distant, demanding and judgmental. This divided view is an idealization. God *is* what I require God to be, and any indication to the contrary must be shoved away out of sight. This is very popular within some church fellowships, especially those devoted to 'claiming the victory' and 'rejoicing always,' which run the danger of denying the presence of darkness and difficulty.

My God?

Suppose that in spite of her experiences the wounded one becomes attracted to or even convinced of the existence of God, and of the love still being revealed in the life and death and resurrection of Jesus Christ—what is she going to make of the claims of Christian tradition that God is omnipresent, omniscient, omnipotent and benevolent?

Abused children often become very compliant and want to be 'good.' They may long for an ideal figure that will always be there and always protect them, and this 'omni-God' gives the wounded one everything she needs for a while. She will think that God must be a loving presence in the world, and that she is forgiven out of the goodness of God's heart for all her undoubted selfishness and failures. It comforts her to think there is someone of infinite resource and goodness 'in charge' of the unpredictable and frightening universe. She is relieved by the temporary lifting of the burden of guilt. She both longs for and recoils from an awareness of being loved perfectly.

She both longs for and recoils from an awareness of being loved perfectly

This intellectual conviction may be a good start. It may be safe and unthreatening enough to be managed. God may be kept securely in a box, a very helpful resource in coping with the struggles and challenges of everyday life. This God teaches patience in stress, hope in difficulty, kindness and self-control as guiding principles, and will never turn his back on her. This God will not manipulate her, nor take advantage of her vulnerability. This God is not like human beings. Some

Her whole identity is bound up with her suffering, and she cannot imagine who she will be

knowledge of the unconditional love of God is essential for the wounded one—the love that will always be there for her as long as she chooses to accept it—if she is to step out on the tightrope that is the genuine walk of faith. She has to have experience already that God loves her enough to die for her, and that this God of the resurrection will never let her go. The wounded one must be confident that 'Underneath are the everlasting arms.' But this God is also kept at more than one remove from the heart of shame and distress. There is a deep division between what can be affirmed with the mind and the will and with even part of the heart, and what is kept locked away in a place hidden from the soul herself.

The wounded one may believe in this 'good' God. Nevertheless the real risk involved in facing the depth of her pain, which even now she is sensing as it shifts behind the closed doors of her awareness, may cause her to refuse the invitation of the Holy Spirit at this point. She may tell herself, firmly, that there is no possibility of finding freedom from the pain. She may believe that her experiences have made her the person she is, and that she knows no other way of being, so removal of the pain is impossible. Her whole identity is bound up with her suffering, and she cannot imagine who she will be or how she will go on if this goes from her. At this stage, 'resurrection' resides on a distant planet called theology and cannot, must not, be made real in the fabric of her life.

The Divided Heart

In the centre of the spiritual difficulties of those wounded by the wickedness or carelessness of others, or by the sheer bloodiness of the human condition, is this sense of dividedness. It is division between everyday awareness and what we might call the true state of things. It is division also between two paradoxical statements of the nature of God's love. It is not that the wounded one necessarily doubts any of the central tenets of faith, but that she becomes increasingly aware that something else is going on under the surface. Something unnameable, but definitely menacing, is stirring. The divisions between conscious thought and hidden images of God, between the light and dark aspects of God, begin to produce an inward tension which becomes increasingly uncomfortable.

Of course, all Christians know that the God of light and love offers love as a free gift through faith in the redeeming work of Jesus Christ on the cross. This God offers forgiveness for the refusals to live in the centre of God's loving will that are the daily experience of every Christian. God lifts the burden of failure and cleanses the wounded from wrong-doing, provided she asks for this relief. This God offers presence through all the vicissitudes of life, and protection from harm, and has an intimate personal concern for the believer and all her doings, albeit at some distance. This God hears and answers prayer, is pleased by the believer's worship, and invites her to an ever more perfect life. But all this is accepted in the conscious parts of the psyche. At a deeper level other factors, other forces are at work which do not understand or accept this God at all. The will has accepted the invitation of Jesus Christ to salvation; but the heart and the memory are still disconnected and darkened by isolation and pain.

The heart and the memory are still disconnected and darkened by isolation and pain

The Gift of Anger

Anger gets a very bad press in the Bible—see the letter of James for example. And it is the human emotion that 'good' children do not have. Anything that is wrong with them or with their lives is their own fault, and our sovereign God graciously forgives when it unfortunately arises, providing one is penitent. So the teaching goes, and so in fact it is. And here the wounded one becomes stuck, often for many years, unable to acknowledge the depth and force of her anger. Owning the impotent fury which is the legacy of abuse must be followed by an immediate willingness to surrender it in penitence and faith, trusting in the forgiveness of God. If she admits to it she must also repent of it.

Now this anger is important. It has held her together psychologically for many years, providing as it does the only internal evidence that the wounded one is a survivor and is innocent of blame for the wrongs that have been done to her. The anger is her only witness to the invisible crimes against her, and the only defendant of the inward place that could never be reached by the invasion of another. It is the only thing which states in the most oblique fashion that she is an individual, a human person created in the image of God, and that she is therefore of infinite value. Her conscious mind loathes herself but the anger asserts her worth. To let go of the anger at this stage, before any healing of the damage that has been done to her, is impossible. So, for as long as is necessary, the wounded one denies her anger, turning it upon herself in depression and self-

Her conscious mind loathes herself but the anger asserts her worth

loathing. It may find release in self-harming behaviours of many different kinds. Since these are inherently sinful, damaging again what God has so lovingly created and redeemed, the wounded one reinforces her self-hatred. She can never be perfect, never be what is apparently required by God and church.

For Christians, there is an understanding that the only allowable form of anger is a righteous one; one that is indignant at the turning of a place of prayer into a market-place; one that is willing to fight against injustice on behalf of the powerless. The wounded one is not going to see her own anger as falling into this category, even though it does. Nor is she likely to think that the God who made her has given her the gift of anger in order to defend herself against psychological disintegration. For some this anger may turn into a complete loss of faith. Innumerable examples can be found through western history of those who have suffered some devastating event and have turned away from God, not because of the event itself but because they have not been able to reconcile the love of God with their own personal suffering. In fact it is possible to see the whole rise of existentialism, with its depressive loss of meaning and its consequent atheism, in post-war Europe as precisely such an occurrence. This God, who allows unspeakable things to happen, is too awful to believe in, never mind offer one's life to in love and service.

For Christians, there is an understanding that the only allowable form of anger is a righteous one

Where is God?

3

This is a very frightening place to be.

The wounded Christian is now in the place of greatest risk, where the choice for faith or atheism has to be made. Some choice is imperative because the inward tensions are too great to live with for any length of time. Wise friends, who can live with both the questions and the anger, will often be the face and the voice of a loving God during this period. A worshipping community that will not reject her can minister some healing of her shame, simply in their acceptance of her. And Scripture may be another friend too, though only if used appropriately. The kind of Scripture reading that simply reinforces the reader's tendency to self-loathing and the pursuit of perfectionism is a gross distortion of the 'word of truth.'

The book of Job presents a masterly evocation of depressive illness. Job's suffering has been immense, and God has specifically permitted this, so we are told. For 37 chapters we read of Job's misery, the grotesquely inadequate answers of his counsellors, and his final determination to call God to account. Like the wounded one, he inflicts further damage to himself—'He took a potsherd with which to scrape himself and sat among the ashes…When [his three friends] saw him from a distance they did not recognize him' (Job 2.8, 12). He wishes he had never been born. God, it seems, is angry with him but will not tell him why. He is penitent of any wrong-doing but still his suffering continues, and he is sure 'that the hand of the Lord has done this' (Job 12.9). Job thinks he must have sinned grossly in order to have deserved such suffering, but in his heart of hearts he knows he has not. He has pursued what he understands as righteousness, and it is not enough to protect him from the anger of God as expressed in the terrible events that have befallen him. As people are still asking, why do good people suffer?

If he could blame himself for his pain, then that would give him a perverse kind of comfort

If he could blame himself for his pain, then that would give him a perverse kind of comfort, even though it would cast God in very harsh light indeed. It would be a simple case of cause and effect. But he cannot lie to himself in this way, 'until I die I will not put away my integrity from me. I hold fast my righteousness, and will not let it go; my heart does not reproach me for any of my days' (27.5–6). He cannot put right what he has not done wrong in the first place; he cannot, no matter what he does, remove the heavy hand of God. When God apparently remains deaf to his pleas he longs for a kinsman-redeemer, someone who would both plead his cause with the Almighty and question him. He wants answers and he wants the pain to stop.

Here the wounded one sees a reflection of her own helplessness in the face of devastating events. She neither had the ability to prevent what happened to her, nor can she understand why God allowed it to happen. Where was God when the abuser came to her in the darkness? Where was God looking when her vulnerability left her open to the violence of another? Did God not see her body violated and her soul terrified? Does the God of love not care what happened to her? The only answer is that, unlike Job, she must be a bad person, for God to be so indifferent to her suffering. But what kind of God does that demonstrate? It is certainly not what she might think of as a God of love.

She neither had the ability to prevent what happened to her, nor can she understand why God allowed it to happen

During all this time God is silent and hidden from Job. The wounded one sees here a reflection of her own present experience. It is wilderness. It is the ash-heap. Pain and questions until she is sick of them, and ready to believe that everyone else is sick of her too. The divine presence moves out of her awareness, echoing the earlier time when the damage was done to her, and the ones to whom she should have been able to look for protection and comfort were not there. But Job tells her she is not alone. Her emptiness and fear have been known by others, she shifts uncomfortably from her belief in a bright shiny God to awareness of a dark and terrible God and back again, in the vain hope of finding a safe resting-place. Her convictions are ambivalent and her personality is brittle. Minor events trigger explosions of anger or massive withdrawal. The absence of the divine is stripping away her irreconcilable images of God.

A Safe Place

This period can be rather like the forty years of the Israelites trudging around the wilderness searching for the Promised Land. She does not know how long it is going on for; she just wishes it could come to an end but fears that this may be what life will be like for evermore. The spiritual diet is thin, for old ways of meeting with God are being removed. Media other than words may be helpful, especially when facing the worst of the pain. Paintings, music, flowers and plants, landscape, water, stones and so forth may become the means whereby she senses that God has not abandoned her. These material things can lift her out of her preoccupations and re-connect her with her physicality. They give her space, offering themselves to her attention, but they never move towards her, threatening violation or pain. It may be the desert, but it will never attack her, and she can survive as she has always managed to do. It may not be comfortable but it feels safe, and surviving, just surviving physically and psychologically, is what she has always done. And as she plods onward there is a tiny movement within, a small but highly significant shift. She senses that there may, just may, possibly be a peace beyond her sufferings—a land of milk and honey.

She cannot go back to what she was before so the choice is either to turn her back on God or continue travelling with him

Nevertheless, there may be powerful temptations to give up on the journey, but she cannot go back now to what she was before so the choice is either to turn her back on God or to continue travelling with him. Other gods occasionally seem attractive, and over-consumption of various kinds may satisfy the aching hole within for a while, but this obviously brings its own malaise with it. Food, shopping, alcohol, drugs of one kind or another, obsessive thoughts and other compulsive behaviours—all these may appeal as a means of controlling the situation. Her relationships with other people may move from intense intimacy to a disappearing act and back again, as she struggles to find her longings answered and her fears assuaged.

To sit in the silence may sometimes be very uncomfortable, as the wounded one no longer knows who she is, nor who God is. Her sense of herself is like an open wound which she does not want touched by others. But nor does she want it ignored by them either. Her mind is edged with pain, its walls raw and bleeding. A mind-dominated theology will now have little to say to her and she may turn aside angrily from its emotional emptiness, for the pain claims all her attention. Contempt, frustration and rebellion all rise easily to the surface—the occasion for more self-loathing. Now she is often pushed and pulled around by all sorts of feelings that she knows are not being triggered by her everyday life, and they can bewilder her. She may tell herself she is stupid, over-emotional and weak, and so may other people, especially those who are not at home with their own emotional lives.

A mind-dominated theology will now have little to say to her

Which Way?

The wounded one is still in the wilderness. Life goes on, forty days or forty years, she does not care much. There are two possibilities. Only two. To carry on, or not. The wounded one may have to make a definite choice for life. She can see the darkness within her and around her, and it may seem very attractive just to abandon herself to its embrace—to give up on God, to give up on all that makes life so difficult, to stop trying to make sense of it all.

As the Israelites near the Promised Land Moses sets before them the choice they must make too. '...I have set before you life and death, blessings and curses. Choose life...loving the Lord your God, obeying him and holding fast to him; for that means life to you and length of days...' (Deuteronomy 30.19–20). She hears his words echoing in her own psyche. Before, she was conscious of believing in a bright shiny God, but now she sees a God of death and darkness, with only small glimmers of light and life. Is this a God she wants to believe in? The thoughts and feelings and questions become a treadmill, forever turning, with no escape but stepping off into death or resigning herself to the limits of the daily round. Frustrated, she moves towards futility.

The thoughts and feelings and questions become a treadmill, forever turning

And there may be other circumstances in her present life which are increasing the inward tensions. So many of them, so powerfully felt, that it may feel as if she is being squeezed through the neck of a bottle, as it were, as the pressures increase. A decision has to be made. Choosing death can seem an attractive option, providing she does not carry very punitive images of God, nor a conviction that the horrors of hell will definitely be visited upon her. Oblivion, the long sleep, would relieve the pain. But by now she also knows that in death she would lose much else. All that is good and positive in her present life will be lost. All the relationships she values, not least her relationship with God, all the people and the places and the experiences would be gone. In all this she may become aware of the Holy Spirit in the darkness; a glimmer that will not be extinguished. The Spirit holds her in her distress, and is not shocked by her excesses of emotion or action, nor angry with her. In the darkness the Spirit offers a velvet warmth as she contemplates the cold waters of death.

The Spirit holds her in her distress, and is not shocked by her excesses of emotion or action, nor angry with her

So she makes the choice for life, though not all who suffer in this way can do this. The damage and the pain are too great for them, but perhaps the Spirit—

the Spirit of love and hope and healing—will still bear them company on the desolate journey they make. But she accepts the invitation to life. She accepts it even though it may seem to be only the obligations of motherhood, or the possible distress of others that call her back from the brink. Where other people seem not to be faced with the question of life or death in the same way, for the wounded one it becomes a definite turning point. From this moment onwards she will accept the journey wherever it may take her. She knows now for certain that her life is the gift of God, a gift which has been restored to her and which she may not dispose of. Her existence is meant. It is intended by God that she be the person she is, and she is to begin to love that person as God loves her.

4   The Saviour Comes

Perhaps it is no accident that the Scriptures which resonate so clearly for the wounded one at this point are those of the Hebrew Bible.

The story of a people chosen but disobedient, suffering but knowing a life-giving joy too; a people who struggle and journey, a people whose lament cries out for the healing power of God. The Psalms give voice to her pain, and provide companions on the way. They also speak of the profound commitment the Lord has made to his people, and his faithfulness especially when in the wilderness. The whole of Psalm 27 speaks of her predicament and of the continuing presence of the Lord in it, offering the possibility of hope.

> The Lord is my light and my salvation; whom shall I fear? The Lord is the stronghold of my life; of whom shall I be afraid? When evil-doers assail me to devour my flesh—my adversaries and my foes—they shall stumble and fall...I believe that I shall see the goodness of the Lord in the land of the living. Wait for the Lord; be strong and let your heart take courage; wait for the Lord.

He may not have been there when she was wounded, but he is here now, and that is a source of hope which gives strength for the journey.

But it is later in Scripture that the hope starts to take on a concrete form in the person of Jesus Christ. His encounters with the damaged and disturbed, in some of whom she sees herself reflected with some accuracy, offer the possibility of healing even now. She knows that the word of Scripture is living and active, that the Lord uses it still to transform the lives of those who read it with open hearts. Indeed she finds that as she begins to meditate on the stories in the gospels that her heart is touched: she is met in the place of isolation and desolation and the feelings that have been hidden inside for many years begin to emerge in the safety of his presence.

She knows that the word of Scripture is living and active

One of the most significant of these stories is that of the woman who bleeds (Luke 8)—though all the accounts of Jesus' meeting with women affirm the value of womanhood to him. For the wounded one, who has thought her womanhood was a liability or nothing more than a source of shame, this acceptance is in itself a healing.

Enclosed in the story of Jairus' daughter, this account of the woman who bleeds speaks directly to her sense of shame. Stigmatized and excluded by her embarrassing and uncontrollable state, she comes to Jesus from behind, where he cannot see her, and touches the fringe of his clothes. She does not want to be noticed because in her experience notice usually leads to further shame and rejection. Her condition means that she will make him ritually unclean by her touch, and there is nothing she can do about that, but he still represents hope to her—maybe her last hope.

Who knows what she felt about the fact that she was suffering from this humiliating condition. Did she question God, like Job, in the long hours of loneliness? Did she rail against him, or shrug her shoulders in resignation? Was it the will of God that she should suffer this? Or was it her own fault— some past transgression the cause of her present trouble?

She had had ten years to reflect on it—years maybe of bitterness and resentment, of physical pain and exhaustion. Years of anger at her helplessness, despite having done all she could to get rid of her shame, despite having given all her money to those who claimed to be able to cure her, but who were in reality just as powerless as she was herself. Perhaps now she had moved beyond all of it, to a place of no feeling at all and no hope, deadened within, until another healer comes to town. And he—what does he do? Does he draw her to one side, as he does with some others who come for his healing, knowing how ashamed she feels? Does he sit down quietly with her alone, to answer her questions and enfold her in a new awareness of the love of God?

The wounded one sees it all in her mind's eye—sees herself as the shamed woman, cut off from others by the unspeakable things that have happened to her and then sees the Christ turn to the woman, demanding that she be exposed for all to see. There was to be no more hiding away, no more pretence that all was well, really. There was to be no collusion between the Anointed One of God, and the religious and social attitudes that kept her isolated and increased her shame. He insisted on bringing her out onto centre stage, into the gaze of all those who had shunned her with their remarkable lack of compassion. His action meant that her shame, the shame of humiliation not of penitence, was no longer to be the controlling force in her interior life. The power has gone forth from him, to heal her physical state, drawn forth perhaps by the silent pleading of her heart, but that is not enough for him. She must own her actions, be a grown-up, acknowledge how it is with her—and hold her head up high. The wounded one knows that if he had let the woman remain hidden then the spiritual dis-ease, the shame of humiliation, would have remained untouched and unhealed. While the shame of penitence leads to release, the shame

If he had let the woman remain hidden then the spiritual dis-ease would have remained untouched and unhealec

of humiliation can only lead to continued captivity. Uncomfortable though it was, it was his love which had restored the woman to wholeness. He knew her concealment was important without being told, he cared enough to do something about it, and he had the power and the desire to do so.

The story offers the wounded one the first hint of the possibility of resurrection—of a new life in which the experiences of the past are not forgotten or discarded, but which might be filled now with the presence of Christ. She opens her heart to the movement of the story, to the movement of Christ within. She hears his word to her of deliverance from shame. The past becomes charged with life not death. The remembrance of hurt and humiliation is no longer empty of love. It is lit from within by Jesus. Memory now holds the possibility of further healing and of a greater restoration to life. It is more than a simple restoration though, for in this new life she will begin to know herself and God more fully than ever before, and already there is a joy that contrasts completely with her earlier experience. Through the story of the humiliated and rejected woman, Christ himself has touched her wounded place and begun the process of healing. Christ himself is present within the wounded place at last.

The Christ Within

It is a truism for Christians that Christ himself comes to dwell within them when they accept him as Saviour. For those who have been violated or humiliated this may be difficult to accept until they can see it as simply a reassurance that they are loved by God, whatever their past may hold, however bad they may be as individuals. But now the wounded one senses this new movement of Christ within, reaching into places that she has never allowed him to enter before, and it is worrying. She realizes that he will never act in an invasive or abusive manner towards her, but the habit of self-defence will not be easily laid aside. Although she senses that he is on the side of the powerless and the captive his felt presence within her most vulnerable place still raises her anxiety levels. No-one else has ever been allowed to see or enter this place. She knows he will never take advantage of his greater resources to move within her without her permission, but at every such movement within there is the barrier of self-protection to be dealt with.

She reflects on Jairus' daughter. The child has reached the point of death when Jesus comes to her. She hears his voice and responds, life is restored and she is fed by those who love and care for her. Something—an illness or injury of some kind—has brought her to this place and now, through Christ's word, she is being offered life again. But she must make the choice to take it. She must rise and put the food into her own mouth. She must do what it takes to hold onto the life she has been given, and to grow into maturity. The past must be left behind and the present lived and the future embraced.

She must do what it takes to hold onto the life she has been given , and to grow into maturity

But it is difficult. Very difficult. For the wounded one it will take time and practice to abandon the controlling mental habits of a lifetime, habits which long ago ensured life but which now lead her to spiritual death because they will always try and shut Jesus out of her soul. Now, she realizes that his love is perfect and that he will only ever work with her best interests at heart, but the struggle to trust remains. However much she knows that, unlike other human beings, his love will contain no element of self-interest or self-promotion, it still takes time and effort to say 'yes,' to allow the divine movement within. The gift of hope and the experience of healing both tell her that he will confront the forces which still imprison her, and he will do so only at the precise moment at which she can face and accept the release which he offers. But it is hard to trust him nevertheless. His manner is gentle, responsive and tender. His love is given in a transparent and uncomplicated way. She does not choose mistrust, but she is still imprisoned by habit, and by something more, something that remains elusive.

This is no easy ride. It is not a luxurious wallowing in the self, but her previous experiences of his healing give her hope that this way lies life. To close down, to turn from what Christ is doing in her remains a constant temptation. And he is challenging. Jesus is truth and he refuses to accept the wounded one's own estimation of herself. He will not accept damage or disturbance as defining a person. They are not the last word or the sum total of who a person is. He calls each one by name, not by the label of her particular need. So he rejects the limits and the lies which the wounded one has used about herself and the world in order to survive. She can no longer pretend that she is not a victim. She must, like the woman who bleeds, acknowledge the nature and extent of her injury and the suffering it has caused her. Jesus can hold her pain. He is not overwhelmed or horrified by it.

Her eyes are being opened, slowly and gently, and the lies are being replaced by truth

In the same way, she can no longer hold onto the idea that the world is a completely uncaring place, nor that there is no love for her in particular. Jesus himself has demonstrated a real love for her, and she sees now that there have always been individuals who have plainly offered her support, refuge or encouragement—all of them forms of love. And there may be particular people around her now, who can speak of hurtful things with gentleness and care, and who by their very presence can assure her that the world is not empty of real love. Her eyes are being opened, slowly and gently, and the lies are being replaced by truth.

The Wound of Love

5

So for months and years, the wounded one has trodden the path of pain, mixed with surprising moments of joy and unexpected gifts of love.

Time passes, allowing her to receive more and more fully the healing that has been worked in her. Her days are ordinary, filled with the usual tasks of life, and the wounded one has a greater sense of peace with herself than she has known before. She meditates upon the stories of encounter with Jesus in the gospels. She hears for herself the words of challenge—do you want to be made well?—and of hope—you, Lord, have the words of eternal life.

But Jesus has not finished his work in her. Much has been accomplished, much has been faced and owned, much has been healed, but freedom still eludes her. Something within is moving again. She thinks of it as a monster in the deep, and is afraid. Jesus, it seems, is determined to disturb it and oust it. There is fear—terror—and there is love too. His love seems so persistent and so patient, so determined to bring her to a place of healing, so willing to go at her own pace, not forcing her but not allowing evasion either. She begins to consider the suffering he endured in his own mortal life.

His love seems so persistent and so patient, not forcing her but not allowing evasion either

Painfully she recognizes that he too was a victim. It hurts, reminding her as it must of her own victimhood, and of how trapped she has been by this, even as she tried to deny it, to 'get on with her life.' Yet for him it was a chosen state. He chose to turn his feet towards Jerusalem. He chose to stay in the city. He knew what Judas was up to and he knew the human frailty of his companions. He chose to go to the Garden as he always did. He chose to allow capture. He surrendered himself to human violence and refused to use it himself. He gave his body to be brutalized. He was imprisoned by ropes and chains, bound before Pilate. He gave up his power and became weak, undefended and open to the physical violation of wicked men. Everything in the wounded one cries out against it. No, no, don't do this—as if in reading it now, she could turn him away from his chosen course, turn him away from the horror of powerlessness, unable to defend himself or to prevent the horrors to come. She wants to rescue him, to save him from a kind of suffering that she knows only too well, that of being held helpless by another and injured by them. As she sees him in her mind's eye, bound, helpless, violated, she sees that he is at one with her. There is nothing in her experience that he has not known himself. He has plumbed the depth of her suffering, her humiliation, her physical hurt. He has gone there with her. And he has done it not because he had to but because he chose to, for love of her. And he is not destroyed by it.

Jesus was a victim, and now she must admit that she was too

Jesus was a victim, and now she must admit that she was too. She can no longer pretend that she was not weak and helpless then, and that within her is still the weak and helpless child. Yes, she is strong now too. She is able to defend herself in most situations, and is very careful not to get herself into situations where she cannot be in sufficient control to stay safe. But behind the strength, the control and the mistrust is still a frightened and vulnerable child, a child that Jesus now accompanies. He was not there, long ago, when she needed him to rescue her, but now in her memory he is there. And he is going to survive.

She continues, with a bravery she did not know she possessed. Perhaps it was possible that he *was* there at the time, but refused to use violence to stop what was happening. He would not use the very instrument that was being employed against one (millions) of his beloved children, for that would only increase the power of violence, and in any case, was completely against his nature. So he 'allowed it to happen,' weeping the while, just as the wounded one now weeps for the suffering that Jesus endured. It is the human condition. It is what people do to one another all the time. Sometimes it is obvious, as in wars and assaults of all kinds. Sometimes it is concealed, hidden behind veils of politeness and respectability. And every time, Jesus weeps. Every time he is there alongside, within the suffering ones, offering them his strength, his own life. Come with me, climb up on my wagon, hitch yourself to my star, and my life will be your life, and you will not be defeated or destroyed either. You will know resurrection just as I did. You will live your life with me because I have lived my life with you.

So he 'allowed it to happen,' weeping the while, just as the wounded one now weeps

At last the wounded one is able to acknowledge fully that she was a victim at the hands of another. The thing so long denied in order to stay 'strong' is owned and the pain of it felt again. But this time it is pain borne in the company of another, one who chooses to identify himself with her, and to stay with her, and to promise her freedom from the past.

It has been a revelation. She is exhausted, but relieved; drained, but released from the need to pretend she is not weak too. But there is more.

She sees the Christ, bound, helpless and weak, having abandoned his divine power so as to be at one with mortals in their bondage to helpless suffering. Her pain is real, present again now, and she sees him standing there, not just human but divine too. Here is Christ the Son of God. Here is the one who spoke the world into being. Here is the one who created a universe in which *her* suffering is possible. She sees the soldiers bend over him with whips and weapons, the sweat on their bodies forced out by the physical effort of beating a human being. And something in her is gleeful. It rushes to the surface, monstrous, powerful and free. Her fury has no bounds. There, she cries, now you know what it is like. Now you suffer too and I am glad. She reaches, as it were, for the whips, and joins in the scourging of his body. *Now you suffer and I am glad.* It is what you deserve for making it possible for me to suffer, not just me but millions of other children, millions of adults too.

The anger which has defended her for so long, but which has also entrapped her in the past, is released

The anger which has defended her for so long, but which has also entrapped her in the past, is released. At the same moment she is horrified. This is not what a 'nice' person does. This is not how a faithful Christian person responds to the suffering of Christ. Her first reaction, of empathy with the suffering Christ, and of gratitude to him— those were the correct responses. Where has all this hatred come from? Could it be that she is not the 'good' person she has always tried to be.

But it has all been too powerful for her to deny. She cannot pretend that she has not hated Christ, that she has not wanted to punish him, to rejoice, to glory in his pain. *Now you know what it is like and I am glad.* It is a million miles from the orthodoxies of repentance and gratitude, but it is honest. It is the truth of what has lain within her soul, hidden in the depths but ready to rise and strike when disturbed. The monster has surfaced, and can never be denied again. The fury will attack even God when the wounded soul is threatened beyond bearing.

But this time it is love which has aroused the rage. Love has reached within and given her permission to exact vengeance on the one ultimately responsible for human suffering, on Christ himself. It is a Pauline moment of revelation. She is both victim and perpetrator. She is both sufferer and one who visits her suffering upon another in revenge. She is a human being, who cannot ultimately control either herself or her surroundings. She is a human being who knows both the inclination to love and the drive to destroy.

The two faces of God are reconciled

And Jesus is both human being and divine. He is identified both with the helpless sufferer and with the omnipotent creator. She holds the two faces of Jesus and her own two faces in her hands. She sees Jesus at one with the powerless and recognizes that she is at one with his accusers. He is victim and she is violent. She is victim and he is love. The two faces of God are reconciled. The fury and the depth of pain behind it are owned. She forgives God and God forgives her.

Revenge or Justice?

These revelations could not be of greater significance to the wounded one. Christ has taken her by the hand, for years, taking her to places within herself and him that she had not known existed. At many places along the way she has needed to stop and rest, or to dig in her heels and resist, or simply to run away from the truth that would set her free.

However, she has arrived at a place of choice. She goes back and replays the momentous events, wanting to hang on to them, to allow them to reach every part of her mind and spirit. The feeling of revenge was sweet, and seductive. Hatred is easy, at least in the short-term, even hatred of God when you have sufficient reason for it, and he seems to exert no pressure at all on her to turn away from it. After all it was entirely justified. She had been wronged, and she had seen God as ultimately responsible for that wrong, since he had created a world in which human beings had the choice to do such things to each other. Gradually though it dawns on her that exacting vengeance is a very narrow path to take and it leads only to a dead end. She wants to keep feeling self-righteously angry, and to glory in punishing God. The child in her thinks she has got away with breaking the rule of unchanging adoration of God. She feels free. The adult in her though, begins to see the limitations of revenge. It can only destroy relationship, and it closes down the possibilities for the future. To break free was one thing, to continue in hatred is quite another. Judging God without mercy will kill the new life waiting to be brought forth.

To break free was one thing, to continue in hatred is quite another

Revenge feels like justice, but it is not. The God who has accomplished all this in her, and in the universe, holds out another promise. Let go of the desire for revenge and you will see justice being done. I will make sure that

justice is done to others, but you must hand over your own seeking of revenge. Only in this way will you be free to live the life I have for you. God
alone is Judge.

To let go of revenge, of self-righteous anger, brings her again to a feeling of
vulnerability. Anger, because it is powerfully felt, gives the illusion of strength,
but it is only illusion. And, if she changes, if she lets go of the past, how will
she still be herself? How can she let go of what has so shaped and informed
her personality? She may repeat the demand to be free of pain, instead of
being willing to accept whatever God gives. She may have great difficulty in
believing that the future can be better than the past. The risk of faith resur-
faces, and she must choose between forgiveness, and continuing to live in
the limbo of Holy Saturday, clinging to the past and devoid of concrete hope
for the future. Eventually, in the time of her own choosing, she opts for forgiveness. She chooses life.

Resurrection

The wounded one has experienced much emotion; she has felt the love of
Christ and owned her fury. Often now she feels nothing, needing to distance
herself from the possibility of more pain, or worse, of joy, or of personal
change. She knows this last to be beyond her: if change is to be wrought in
her only Christ can do it. In the face of life she may be tempted by death once
again, longing for the darkness of the tomb with Jesus. But he is no longer
there.

He appears to Mary Magdalen and the other women, and the wounded one
sees the love he has for them, the affirmation he gives in coming to them
first. He appears to Thomas, and she sees the struggle to have faith, to believe in a transformed and transforming future. She may still be angry at the
grief and the suffering. She may wish God had thought of a better plan for
human beings, one that did not seem to involve all this suffering. But then,
that is what we chose. Above all, perversely, she fears hope itself. She has
chosen life, but is terrified of the challenges
it will bring. She wobbles uncertainly between strong confidence that all will be well,
and a weakness that dreads well-being. In
the tension her feelings become deadened;
am I weak or am I strong—or am I something beyond and more than either of those
things?

*Am I weak or am I strong
—or am I something
beyond and more than
either of those things?*

Somewhere in the resurrection accounts, resurrection comes to her, when
she is able to receive it. A dawning realization that God is beyond and within

25

everything. The Holy Trinity embracing the world and the whole of creation in an intense and powerful love, before which resistance, rebellion and reluctance are completely irrelevant. It is there, whatever the human response may be. It is there and once received can never be denied. All are drawn into this love, whether they will or no. There can be no resisting it in the end, whatever the individual soul may think. The love pours out in truth and judgment, in a passionate caring that transcends all else. The love cannot be destroyed by humans; it is immense and free. All are caught up in its power—the lonely child, the damp and dismal adult, the violent and the violated, the offender and the offended against. The wounded one is overwhelmed, but this time with joy and gratitude. She knows herself both puny and cherished, as is the world in which she lives, and she is able at last to rejoice in the fact.

> *The love pours out in truth and judgment, in a passionate caring that transcends all else*

The love that has cared for her throughout the whole journey of her life is revealed at last in something closer to its true nature and dimensions. Human life, her life, with all its pain and its joy, is gift. Before this love she is nothing, and only becomes something insofar as God gives her life and breath and worth. She registers the generosity of that gift of life, and the beauty of the world in which she may live it to the full. She acknowledges, maybe with some difficulty still, the blessing of God's love, and is aware that this new knowledge will itself transform her life from now onwards. She can do nothing but say yes—or no, as she wishes. Love will do it. It will present her spotless before God, now and always. There she will know and be fully known.

The Wound of Love

The wounded one has travelled far. In the depth of her being she is a new creation, and she need no longer think of herself as the wounded one. The damage done to her is being healed. The damage done by her is forgiven. She is beloved, and now she knows this. Perhaps though, as she reflects on all that has happened, she may see that she has in fact been wounded again, in precisely the same unnameable place as before, but this time she has received the wound of love. The delicate surgery of the divine hand uncovered her unhealed hurt, cutting open the flesh without very much in

> *In the depth of her being she is a new creation, and she need no longer think of herself as the wounded one*

the way of anaesthetic and excising the poisons of hatred and rage. In their place Christ has put his own love, which will continue to stretch and enlarge her heart for the rest of her days. Her whole understanding of herself and of the world is being transformed. The idea of serving others, of offering herself to God and to others in thanksgiving for all that has been given to her, returns with greater force and attraction than ever before.

Often she will want to retreat, to say no, to announce that the difficulty of being more than just a wounded person is too great. She may fear being overwhelmed by what is asked of her. But every time she will hear the words echoing down the years, choose life…

6 Suggestions for Further Reading

For more on the inward journey:

Richard Foster, *Prayer* (Hodder and Stoughton, 1992)

Gerard Hughes, *God of Surprises* (Darton, Longman and Todd, 1985)

Margaret Silf, *Landmarks* (Darton, Longman and Todd, 1998)

For a more obvious theological underpinning:

James Alison, *Faith Beyond Resentment* (Darton, Longman and Todd, 2001)

Alastair V Campbell, *The Gospel of Anger* (SPCK, 1989)

Robert Fyall, *How Does God Treat His Friends?* (Christian Focus Publications, 1995)

Rowan Williams, *Christ on Trial* (Zondervan, 2000)

Rowan Williams, *Resurrection* (Darton Longman and Todd, 1982)